UNDERSTANDING THE
SUNDAY EUCHARIST

*To the memory of
my mother and father*

BRIAN GRENIER CFC

UNDERSTANDING THE SUNDAY EUCHARIST

ALBA · HOUSE   NEW · YORK

SOCIETY OF ST. PAUL, 2187 VICTORY BLVD., STATEN ISLAND, NEW YORK 10314

UNDERSTANDING THE SUNDAY EUCHARIST
© Brian Grenier CFC, 1990

First published, May 1990
Second printing, November 1991

Illustrations: Patricia Murray
Cover design & photo: Bruno Colombari SSP

Nihil Obstat: Rev. Paul Crowley BTh, SLL
Imprimatur: † John Heaps DD, VG,
                    Sydney, NSW
                    28th April 1990

The Nihil Obstat and Imprimatur are a declaration that a book or pamphlet is considered to be free from doctrinal or moral error. It is not necessarily implied that those who have granted them agree with the contents, opinions or statements expressed.

AUSTRALIAN EDITION
Published by
ST PAUL PUBLICATIONS — Society of St Paul,
60-70 Broughton Road — Homebush, NSW 2140

National Library of Australia
Card Number and ISBN 0 949080 61 6

NORTH AMERICAN EDITION
Published by
ALBA HOUSE — Society of St Paul,
2187 Victory Boulevard, Staten Island, New York, 10314-6603
ISBN 0-8189-0639-1

Typeset and printed by Society of St Paul, Wantirna South, Victoria

St Paul Publications and **Alba House** are activities of the Priests and Brothers of the Society of St Paul who proclaim the Gospel through the media of social communication.

Contents

Introduction

TIME, The Weekly Newsmagazine; copyright Time Inc.

Scrutiny—*Trenton Times*, February 1, 1975; interview with Wilson Barto

Hands Tied—*New Times*, June 11, 1976; story by Robert Shrum

Detente—*Time*, May 10, 1976; interview with Dean E. Fischer. Reprinted by permission from TIME, The Weekly Newsmagazine; copyright Time Inc.

Henry Kissinger—*Time*, May 10, 1976; interview with Dean E. Fischer. Reprinted by Permission from TIME, The Weekly Newsmagazine; copyright Time Inc.

Developing Nations-2—*Time*, May 10, 1976; interview with Dean E. Fischer. Reprinted by permission from TIME, The Weekly Newsmagazine; copyright Time Inc.

Jewish Appeal—from an unpublished memo of Shrum's. A virtually identical account by Shrum was published in *New Times*

CHAPTER 10

Balanced Budget—*U.S. News and World Report*, May 24, 1976; interview with John Mashek

Ford's Economy—*Time*, May 10, 1976; interview with Dean E. Fischer. Reprinted by permission from TIME, The Weekly Newsmagazine; copyright Time Inc.

Welfare Mothers—*Harper's*, March, 1976; story by Steven Brill. Carter's staff has conceded that the number of welfare mothers in this program is actually in the hundreds.

Watergate Pardons?—*Time*, May 10, 1976; interview with Dean E. Fischer. Reprinted by permission

1. The reform of the liturgy

The convocation of the Second Vatican Council by Pope John XXIII came as a surprise to almost the entire Church. It was less surprising, given the pastoral orientation of the Council, that the first of its many documents to be promulgated was the *Constitution on the Sacred Liturgy;* for 'the liturgy is the summit toward which the activity of the Church is directed; it is also the fount from which all her power flows' (*SC #10*).

Since the Council, serious attempts have been made to renew and, where necessary, to reform the liturgy of the Eucharist and the other sacraments. This has entailed many changes (not all

8

from TIME, The
Time Inc.
  Abortion—*Bosto*
by Curtis Wilkie
  Abortion-2—*New*
1976
  Arabs—Associate
  Right to Work-3
1976; story by Jim
  National Guard—United Press International, October 27, 1970

equally understandable or even welcome to the faithful); and it has augmented the need for on-going adult catechesis.

Such instruction should help us to see the eucharistic sacrifice of the Mass for what it is — 'the true centre of the whole Christian life both for the universal Church and for the local congregation' *(Eucharisticum mysterium I, B)*. It should also facilitate the 'full, conscious, and active participation in liturgical celebrations which is demanded by the very nature of the liturgy' *(SC #14)*.

This simple instructional booklet, which treats in sequence the various parts of the Mass, is intended to assist Catholics to participate more meaningfully and more fruitfully in the Sunday Eucharist. It collects a series of brief essays which appeared over the course of a year in the weekly parish bulletin of St Paul Publications — *Our Sunday Celebration.*

The booklet will be most useful if it is read in conjunction with a missal of some kind so that frequent reference can be made to the actual text of the Mass. It may be helpful to read (or reread) it, chapter by chapter, over a period of time as part of one's personal preparation for Mass.

2. Personal preparation for Mass

We know well the care we take over tidying the house, setting the table, and preparing a tasty meal when we invite friends to dinner. We know, too, the attention we give to details, large and small, when we are preparing for a significant event in our lives such as a trip overseas or a wedding in our family. Yet we can come to Mass Sunday after Sunday without adverting to the fact that this very significant event in the life of our faith community also calls for detailed and serious preparation.

The task of preparing the sacred space (arranging flowers, hanging banners, 'setting the table', etc.) falls to some people. Others select and practise the hymns which will enhance the celebration. The readers study and rehearse the prescribed liturgical readings; and the priest devotes some hours to the preparation of a homily.

Our own personal preparation for the Eucharist is likewise very important and should begin well before we arrive at the church. We might, for example, spend some time during the week going over the Sunday readings, perhaps with the help of a commentary. Or we might formulate (alone or with the family) the intentions for which we will offer this Mass.

At least, we can see to it that we arrive in good time, greet other members of the parish community and recall God's presence in the assembly before the liturgy begins. If, as may often be the case, we find ourselves preoccupied, let us bring those concerns to the celebration; for what has potential for distraction has potential for prayer.

3. The meaning of the assembly

We come together with other human beings often and for a variety of reasons. However, there is something very special about the group of people which assembles for the Lord's Supper in our parish church.

As Christian believers who have a shared vision of what life is ultimately about and who gather in Jesus' name and in his presence (cf. Mt 18:20), we are conscious of the fact that we are a group with a difference. We are, to reclaim an old phrase, 'a holy communion'.

The parish community, celebrating with a priest the memorial of the Lord or eucharistic sacrifice, is not merely a part of the Church. Our liturgy is truly an action of the whole Church, united in one body with Christ as head. As St Paul reminds us: 'Because there is one loaf of bread, all of us, though many, are one body, for we all share the same loaf' (1 Cor 10:17).

Just as we can use a magnifying glass to focus the sun's rays and to make the sun present with burning intensity in one place, so also does the local liturgical assembly bring together in a mysterious way the entire Church.

The Mass will not mean much to us if other parishioners mean little or nothing to us, if the congregation is an impersonal gathering which prefers restaurant style dining at separate tables to the conviviality of a celebratory banquet.

Let us pray in the words of the second Eucharistic Prayer: 'May all of us who share in the body and blood of Christ be brought together in unity by the Holy Spirit.'

4. *The whole person at prayer*

Anyone who observes a Muslim at prayer will be struck by the number and variety of the prescribed gestures and postures. This should not surprise us; for we do not suddenly become disembodied spirits when we communicate with God. It is perfectly natural for human beings to express their interior sentiments by means of 'body language'.

The bishops of Vatican II had this in mind when they said: 'To promote active participation [in the liturgy], the people should be encouraged to take part by means of acclamations, responses, psalms, antiphons, hymns, **as well as by actions, gestures, and bodily attitudes'** (*SC* #30).

This recommendation has special relevance to Masses that are celebrated with children. For them the liturgy is very much an activity involving the entire person (*DMC* #33-34).

It is so easy, as creatures of habit, just to stand, sit, kneel and make occasional signs of the cross without adverting to why we do these things (cf. *GI* #20-22). This is not to imply that we should act in some self-conscious fashion. 'The art of liturgical gesturing,' writes Mark Searle, 'like the art of etiquette, should be learned so well that it can be forgotten.'

If it does nothing else, the meaningful use of suitably expressive gestures and bodily attitudes emphasises the essentially communitarian nature of liturgical prayer. As the *General Instruction* states: 'The uniformity in standing, kneeling, or sitting to be observed by all taking part is a sign of the community and the unity of the assembly; it both expresses and fosters the spiritual attitude of those taking part' (*GI* #20).

5. Liturgical Singing

Among the various forms that 'full, conscious, and active participation' (*SC #14*) in the liturgy can take, singing is one of the most ancient (see Eph 5:19; Col 3:16) and most worthy of promotion (*MS #16; SC #118*). 'With due consideration for the culture and ability of each congregation,' notes the *General Instruction*, 'great importance should be attached to the use of singing at Mass' (*GI #19*).

Such singing is not just a devotional extra; nor is it an end in itself. It should facilitate our entry as a community of faith into the mysteries which we have come together to celebrate.

Expressing our faith in song can give a 'more noble form' (*MS* #5) to liturgical worship, thereby conferring 'greater solemnity upon the sacred rites' (*SC* #112). At the same time, it can make us more attentive to our prayer and the prayer itself more pleasing (*MS* #5; *SC* #112).

Moreover, as we know from experience, there are few better ways of uniting a group of people than by having them join together in song. This is especially true of festive occasions like the Mass in which 'the unity of hearts is more profoundly achieved by the union of voices' (*MS* #5).

Singing can also increase the effectiveness and 'impact' of the texts we pray, provided that appropriate musical settings are chosen.

The priest, the cantor, the choir and the full assembly all have specific roles to play. However, 'one cannot find anything more religious and more joyful in sacred celebrations than a **whole congregation** expressing its faith and devotion in song' (*MS* #16).

Introductory Rites

6. Entrance procession/ opening song

In times past, when the sacristy of many larger churches was situated near the entrance, the ministers would make their way in solemn procession through the assembled people to the altar. Changes in church architecture led to the abbreviation of this procession; but the old practice is being restored today in many places because of its special significance.

The procession helps to set the scene for the action by highlighting the fact that we are a worshipping people (1 Pet 2:5,9) from whose midst some are called forth and ordained to lead the liturgical celebration.

Traditionally in the Roman Church, the entrance procession was accompanied by the singing of a song — an appropriate psalm, introduced and concluded with an antiphon (a short keynote passage from the text). This is the origin of the entrance antiphon which, depending on local custom, may be recited by the congregation as the ministers enter.

As singing can help us to find and to express our common identity, there is much to recommend a suitable processional hymn sung by the whole congregation, perhaps with the assistance of a choir or a cantor.

Though greater flexibility is permitted these days in the choice of hymns, we should not lose sight of the special function of the song which begins our celebration. The *General Instruction of the Roman Missal* puts it this way:

> *The purpose of this song is to open the celebration, intensify the unity of the gathered people, lead their thoughts to the mystery of the season or feast, and accompany the procession of priests and ministers (GI #25).*

21

7. *Reverence to the altar*

Just as we kiss the cross in the liturgy of Good Friday as a mark of reverence for our Saviour, so also the priest and his attendants pay homage to the altar at the beginning and end of every Mass. They do so because it represents Christ who is the cornerstone (Eph 2:20-22) of God's holy temple which we ourselves are (1 Cor 3:9-17).

Their homage may take the form of a bow (or a genuflection if the tabernacle is located in the sanctuary), the kissing of the altar, and (on particularly solemn occasions) the incensing of the altar.

The kissing of the altar is reminiscent of the ancient pagan customs of kissing the threshold of their temple and, in the presence of their household gods, the family dinner table.

For us the kiss expresses respect for the altar and symbolizes our desire for union with Christ who is, as it were, the host of our sacrificial meal.

Later in the Mass, in a similar spirit of faith and love, we will exchange the kiss of peace with one another as an expression of our union in Christ whose Spirit dwells in us as in a temple (1 Cor 6:19; 2 Cor 6:16).

The incensation of the altar, which is a special feature of liturgies in the Eastern Church, is suggestive of purification and of our prayer ascending before the throne of God (Lev 16:12-13; Ps 141:2; Rev 5:8). It might also symbolize the cloud wherein God's glory was made manifest to the Chosen People (Ex 16:10; etc.).

8. The sign of the cross

When we enter the church, we traditionally make the sign of the cross on our body, using blessed water. Hopefully, we have not reduced to a perfunctory gesture this expressive reminder of our baptism, in the name of the Holy Trinity, into a worshipping community.

The practice of signing oneself with a cross is a very ancient one among Christians. Writing about 211 A.D., Tertullian observed: 'At every action of our day we sign the forehead with the sign of the cross.' We do the same thing at the beginning of the Gospel reading.

Just as slaves had the name of their master tattooed or branded on their forehead (or other visible part of their body), Christians marked or sealed their forehead with the sign of the Lord who is also our Saviour from the slavery of sin (2 Cor 1:22; Eph 1:13; Rev 7:3).

The sign of the cross, devoutly made at the beginning of the Mass (when we bless ourselves) and at the end of the Mass (when we receive a blessing from the priest), is our way of saying that we belong to Christ. It is, moreover, an affirmation of our faith in the saving mystery of Jesus' sacrificial death.

That sacrifice, which Jesus offered once and for all for sin (Heb 10:12), is re-presented in our celebration of the Eucharist.

Finally, this ancient gesture may serve to remind us of the fact that the following of a crucified redeemer is, in the words of Robert Southwell, the English Jesuit martyr, 'a rough profession'.

9. The exchange of greetings

After signing themselves with the cross, the priest and people exchange greetings. This acknowledgment of one another's presence is in keeping with the purpose of the introductory rites, namely 'that the faithful coming together take on the form of a community' (*GI #24*).

Three forms of greeting are given in the Order of Mass in the English missal. The first two are similar to the greetings we find at the beginning and end of Paul's letters (1 Cor 1:3; 16:23; Gal 1:3; 6:18; etc.).

The third form, 'The Lord be with you,' also has its origin in scripture (Ruth 2:4; 2 Thess 3:16; 2 Tim 4:22). We respond, 'And also with you.' This same dialogue will be repeated at the beginning of the Eucharistic Prayer, at the sign of peace, and at the concluding blessing.

In a welcoming gesture, the priest extends his arms as if to embrace all present and to call for their involvement in the sacred rites.

Traditionally, the bishop has used the special form: 'Peace be with you' — the greeting of the Risen Jesus to his discipes (Lk 24:36; Jn 20:19, 21). This recalls Jesus' injunction: 'When you go into a house, say, "Peace be with you"' (Mt 10:12; cf. Lk 10:5).

Whichever form is used, the greeting should direct our thoughts to the presence in our midst of the Lord Jesus who is our peace (Eph 2:14). With this in mind, we will appreciate more fully the words of the *General Instruction of the Roman Missal:* 'This greeting and the congregation's response express the mystery of the gathered Church' (*GI* #28).

27

10. Penitential rite/Kyrie

The inclusion of a penitential rite at this point may help us to approach the Lord's table with a pure conscience and the proper dispositions. As Jesus taught, we should seek reconciliation before we presume to bring our gifts to the altar (Mt 5:23-25).

The missal gives three variants of the rite; but other forms, more in harmony with the liturgical seasons or the readings of the day, are permissible. Some creativity is called for in Masses with particular groups (e.g. children).

Predictably, the rite has four steps: the priest invites us to recall our sins; we reflect in silence; we publicly as a community acknowledge our sinfulness; and the priest prays, asking for God's mercy and forgiveness.

Instead of the usual penitential rite, the *Sacramentary* makes provision at Sunday Masses for the blessing and sprinkling of the people with holy water (cf. Ps 51:7JB). The imposition of ashes on Ash Wednesday serves a like function.

The *Kyrie Eleison* (Lord, have mercy) — the remnant of an ancient litany — follows the penitential rite, unless it has been incorporated into it. It is as much an act of homage to the Risen Lord as it is a cry of repentance and a plea for mercy.

It may be sung in quite a variety of ways, thus ensuring greater participation on the part of the congregation.

Pertinent to all these considerations is the fact that salvation and forgiveness in the Gospels are frequently associated with meals at which Jesus was present (see Lk 7:36-50; 19:2-10; Jn 21:9-14; etc.), especially the Last Supper.

11. Glory to God in the highest

Part of our rich Christian inheritance are the
hymns to be found in the New Testament (Phil
2:6-11; Heb 1:3-4; Col 1:15-20) and in the old
sacramentaries. One of the best known is the
Gloria which is 'an ancient hymn in which the
Church, assembled in the Holy Spirit, praises
and entreats the Father and the Lamb [i.e.
Christ]' (*GI* #31).

Though it begins with the jubilant words of the angels announcing Jesus birth (Lk 2:13-14), it was originally associated not with Christmas but with Easter. Influenced by Jewish prayer models, the *Gloria* came into the Roman liturgy from Eastern sources early in the sixth century as a morning hymn of joyful praise.

At first it was reserved to special occasions (Sundays and martyrs' feasts) and only the bishop might intone it, except at the Easter Vigil when all priests were accorded this privilege. Its use gradually became less exclusive and more widespread; and today we include the *Gloria* at most Masses on Sundays (except during Lent and Advent), solemnities and feasts.

It can be recited by the congregation; but, given the fact that it is a hymn, it calls out to be sung by all present. With a suitable musical setting and with the help of a choir (or cantor), this is surely possible.

Some people may find the sudden change of mood from the penitential rite a little awkward. However, we are doing what comes naturally for the Christian; for, as Chesterton has said, 'Praise should be the permanent pulsation of the soul.'

12. Opening prayer (Collect)

At important transition points in the Mass there is a prayer to be recited by the presiding celebrant. The first of these presidential prayers, which help to set the tone of the day's celebration, is sometimes called the collect because it gathers together the prayers and intentions of the faithful.

Using the words 'Let us pray' or some such invitatory formula, the priest asks the assembly to unite with him in prayer. A mandatory time of silence follows 'so that [we] may realise [we] are in God's presence and may call [our] petitions to mind' (*GI* #32). This is not the silence of a mute spectator but a form of participation (cf. *SC* #30).

Then 'in a loud and clear voice' (*GI* #12) and with his arms outstretched, the priest addresses God, our Father, petitioning him in a rather formal and general way to meet our needs as a community through the mediation of our high priest, Jesus Christ (1 Tim 2:5; Heb 8:6; 9:15; 12:24).

Confident that the Father will give us whatever we ask of him in Jesus' name (Jn 14:13-14; 15:16; 16:23, 26), we give our assent to the prayer by acclaiming, 'Amen'.

The reader is invited to examine some of these presidential prayers (opening prayer, prayer over the gifts, and prayer after communion), noting their structure.

With the recitation of the collect we have come to the conclusion and climax of the introductory rites. The community should now be ready 'to listen to God's word and celebrate the eucharist properly' (*GI* #24).

Liturgy of the Word

13. Liturgy of the Word

The faith which brings us together at Mass 'comes from hearing the message' (Rom 10:17). Not surprisingly, then, like the early Christians, we join scripture reading to our celebration of the Eucharist. Venerating the 'divine Scriptures' as we venerate the Body of the Lord, we 'partake of the bread of life ... from the one table of the Word of God and the Body of Christ' (*DV* #21).

Implicit in the Council Fathers' reference to 'one table ' is an admonition not to devalue the liturgy of the word, as if it were merely a preparation for the liturgy of the eucharist which follows. In another document they assure us that 'the two parts which in a sense go to make up the Mass, viz. the liturgy of the word and the eucharistic liturgy, are so closely connected with each other that they form but one single act of worship (*SC* #56).

We know in faith that, 'when the Scriptures are read in Church, God himself is speaking to his people' (*GI* #9; cf. *GI* #33 and *SC* #7). Hence the minister can say at the end of the reading (not in a literal, fundamentalist sense, however): 'This is the word of the Lord.'

We know also that 'Christ is present to the faithful through his own word' (*GI* #33; cf. *GI* #9; *SC* #7) for our spiritual nourishment. Hopefully, our faith in the 'real presence' of Christ in the Sacrament of the Eucharist does not obscure the reality of his presence in the Church in other ways (see *MF* #36-41).

In the pages which follow, we will consider the elements which together make up the liturgy of the word.

14. First reading

Since the revision of the lectionary in 1969, we now have three readings each Sunday, arranged according to a three year cycle. The first of these, after centuries of neglect, is usually taken from the Hebrew Scriptures (a preferable term to 'Old Testament'). During Easter we follow the very ancient custom of selecting our first reading from the Acts of the Apostles.

We read from those writings which nourished the spiritual life of Jesus himself and his early followers because they have a 'perpetual value' and a 'continuing validity' in their own right. 'All scripture,' as Paul asserts, 'is inspired by God' (2 Tim 3:16).

Our forefathers and foremothers in the faith were well aware of this; and they continued to read the Hebrew Scriptures (in a Greek translation called the *Septuagint*) even after their expulsion from the synagogues in about 90 A.D.

Perhaps we Christians need to take more account of the 'continuity of the work of salvation' (*GI* #318), remembering that God has not abrogated his covenant with the Jews. 'God does not change his mind about whom he chooses and blesses' (Rom 11:29).

We sit while the appointed minister proclaims God's word from the lectern; it is an appropriate posture which should facilitate attention.

At the conclusion of the reading we respond fittingly: 'Thanks be to God.' Our most important response, however, must always be sought in our reflection on what has been read and in our efforts to live out the revealed truth in our daily lives.

15. Silence/Reflection

Among the various ways in which we can actively participate in the Mass, the *Constitution on the Sacred Liturgy* includes the observance of 'a reverent silence' (*SC* #30). Christians of the Quaker tradition would appreciate that; for in their assemblies they speak only when they can 'improve upon the silence'.

Silence is an appropriate form of participation at the penitential rite, after the invitation to prayer ('Let us pray'), at the end of a reading, following the homily, and after communion (*GI #23*). The time set aside for this quiet reflection should be neither too brief nor too long.

Fr Lucien Deiss, the well-known liturgist, makes an interesting distinction between dead silence wherein nothing is happening and living silence 'which is heavily populated by the presence of God.' Obviously, it is the latter that we have in mind in this brief exposition.

It is the kind of silence that we associate with Mary, the mother of Jesus, of whom Luke said: 'Mary remembered all these things and thought deeply about them' (Lk 2:19); and, 'His mother treasured all these things in her heart' (Lk 2:51).

During the times of silence, which are so important in our celebration of the liturgy, we might find it helpful to pray some suitable prayers of our own choosing which relate to the themes of the readings for the day; or it may suit us better just to listen to the words that God speaks in our heart. In Meister Eckhart's words: 'The very best and utmost attainment in this life is to remain still and let God act in thee.'

16. Responsorial psalm

Following the pattern of the morning prayer service in the Jewish synagogue, we respond to the first reading by reciting or singing, wholly or in part, a psalm or other biblical song.

These are the prayers which Jesus himself sang (Mt 26:30; Mk 14:26) and which the resurrected Christ interpreted anew for his disciples (Lk 24:44-45). They were equally dear to the early Christian communities (Jas 5:13; Col 3:16; Eph 5:18-19).

Is there any better way of responding to God's word than by using a prayer which, as Louis Bouyer expresses it, 'continues in the mouth of man to be the Word of God?' The scripture reading speaks *to* us; the psalms speak *for* us (an observation attributed to St Athanasius).

The responsorial psalm is an 'integral part of the liturgy of the word' (*GI* #36); it is 'a unique and very important song' (*MCW* #63) which is designed to help us to reflect on the reading. For this reason, it will ordinarily have some thematic connection to the readings of the day and/or the liturgical season.

Where possible, taking care to avoid routine, the psalm should be sung. Official documentation supports this:

> *The psalmist or cantor of the psalm sings the verses of the psalm at the lectern or other suitable place. The people remain seated and listen, but also as a rule take part by singing the response, except when the psalm is sung straight through without the response. (GI #36).*

As we sing the psalms in the name of the Church, it does not matter if the sentiments expressed are at variance with our own mood at a given time.

17. Second reading

As a result of the Council Fathers' wish that 'the treasures of the Bible [should] be opened up more lavishly . . . for the faithful' (*SC* #51), we now have an expanded lectionary and, on Sundays and feasts, three readings instead of two. (It should be noted that, for pastoral reasons, one of the first two readings may be omitted — *GI* #318).

Though there is usually a clear relationship between the first and third readings, it is often difficult (at least during the many Sundays of Ordinary Time) to harmonize the second reading with either of the others. This can create problems for the overzealous homilist.

The reason that the second readings for Sundays and feasts tend to stand alone is that they have been allocated with a view to more or less continuous reading of the New Testament epistles. For example, during Year A of the three year cycle, St Paul's letter to the Romans is read from the 9th to the 24th Sundays of Ordinary Time.

This reflects the practice of the early Church. As St Justin recorded about 150 A.D., the reader would simply take up where the previous week's reader left off and would read for as long as time allowed.

One advantage of the second reading is that it puts us in touch in a special way with the joyful, sorrowful and glorious mysteries of the lives of the first century Christian faith communities. One with them in the redeeming Christ, we learn from their example, drawing out of the treasure house of their writings new and old insights (Mt 13:52).

18. Gospel acclamation

For many music-lovers, the high point of Handel's *Messiah* is the magnificent 'Alleluia Chorus'. The audience stands to hear it, as King George II did when the *Messiah* was first performed in London.

We, too, stand for the singing of the Alleluia or (during Lent) a similar acclamation of praise at the end of the second reading. This is our 'greeting of welcome to the Lord who is about to speak to [us]' (*LMI* #23).

Despite current practice in many places, the introduction to our revised lectionary (2nd edition, 1981) insists that 'the Alleluia or verse before the Gospel **must be sung ... by the whole congregation together**' (*LMI* #23). If it is not sung, it should be omitted.

The expression 'Alleluia', is to be found in a number of the psalms, sometimes as an introductory cry of joyful praise (see Pss 105-107, 111—114, 116—118) and elsewhere as a rousing conclusion (see Ps 106:48). Its only occurrence in the New Testament is in the triumphant hymn of victory for the wedding day of the Lamb in the Book of Revelation where it is used four times (Rev 19:1,3,4,6). This suggests that 'Alleluia' (i.e. 'praise God') was carried over from Jewish worship into the Christian liturgy fairly early in the piece.

The practice of adding a 'sequence' to the Alleluia, which was not uncommon in the Middle Ages, survives today only in the liturgies of Easter and Pentecost.

Blessed be the Lord, the God of Israel, through all eternity! / Let all the people say, Amen! Alleluia. (Ps 106:48 NAB).

47

19. Gospel

Even a non-Christian visitor would conclude that this is the climax of the liturgy of the word; for 'the liturgy itself inculcates the great reverence to be shown toward the reading of the Gospel, setting it off from the other readings by special marks of honour' (*GI #35*).

Our visitor might note that this reading is reserved for an ordained minister (preferably a deacon), that the people respectfully stand for the proclamation of the good news, that the reader exchanges a greeting with the congregation, that all present sign themselves with three small crosses, that the people direct their acclamations at the beginning and end of the reading to Christ himself, and that the reader kisses the book just as he had earlier kissed the altar.

In more solemn celebrations a beautifully bound and ornamented book of the Gospels may be carried in procession from the altar to the lectern, thereby highlighting the link between the table of the Eucharist and the table of the word of God. To honour Christ, present in his word, lighted candles are carried and the book is incensed. Depending on his own talents and on the literary character of the prescribed reading, the deacon or priest may chant the Gospel.

The bishops at Vatican II gave us a good lead in this regard by solemnly enthroning the book of the Gospels at the beginning of each day's session.

As the priest bows to the altar and prays for purity of heart (Is 6:6-8), let us pray for the grace to hear this saving truth and put it into practice (Jn 5:24).

20. Homily

It was a time-honoured custom, even in Jesus' own day, for someone to comment on the readings in the synagogue service (cf. Lk 4:16-27; Mk 1:21; 6:1-6; Jn 6:59). The early Christians perpetuated this practice (cf. Acts 13); and, during the era of the great Fathers like Augustine and John Chrysostom, the Church witnessed a golden age of liturgical preaching.

In later centuries the homily was devalued somewhat in the mistaken belief that it was just an adjunct to the act of worship, a kind of optional extra. As if to bracket the homily out from the rest of the Mass, the priest would remove his maniple while preaching or otherwise surround it with superfluous ritual.

Vatican II reaffirmed the importance of the homily. Not only should it hold pride of place in the ministry of the word (*DV* #24), it is to be 'highly esteemed as part of the liturgy itself' (*SC* #52) — 'an integral part of the liturgy [which] increases the word's effectiveness' (*GI* #9, cf. *GI* #41).

The *General Instruction of the Roman Missal* requires a homily to be preached at all Masses that are celebrated with a congregation on Sundays and holydays of obligation. 'It may not be omitted without a serious reason' (*GI* #42; cf. *SC* #52).

The preacher should ordinarily be the priest celebrant who 'should develop some point of the readings or of another text from the Ordinary or from the Proper of the Mass of the day' (*GI* #41).

At the conclusion of the homily there should be a period of silent reflection.

51

21. Profession of faith

'The words are few, but the mysteries they contain are awe-inspiring.' These words are addressed to catechumens when, in the rites preparatory to their baptism, they are formally presented with the Church's profession of faith. In reciting this creed, they not only give their assent to the propositions it contains but also publicly affirm their unity in faith, hope and love with the community.

The creed which we pray on Sundays and solemnities (*GI* #44) in the context of the liturgy of the word is actually a transplant from the liturgy of baptism. A summary statement of the key tenets of our Christian faith, as outlined by the Councils of Nicea (325) and Constantinople (381), it came into the Roman Mass only at the beginning of the 11th century.

Using the plural form ('We believe . . .'), as befits a community, we affirm our faith in the word proclaimed in the readings and preached in the homily, recalling those saving mysteries which we will celebrate sacramentally in the liturgy of the Eucharist.

Of course, the great profession of our faith is the Eucharistic Prayer itself wherein we offer thanksgiving to God for the whole work of salvation. We make it our own with a resounding 'Amen'.

When we pray the Creed, it is recommended that we bow at the words, 'by the power of the Holy Spirit. . .' (*GI* #98). A genuflection is preferred on the feasts of the Annunciation and Christmas. Finally, we might note that, in Masses celebrated with children, the simpler Apostles' Creed may be used (*DMC* #39, 49).

22. General intercessions

At the conclusion of the liturgy of the word, in a spirit of 'deep solidarity with the human race and its history' (*GS #1*), we present our general intercessions to the Father through Christ, our Lord.

The importance of this very 'catholic' element in our liturgy (restored to the Mass after a millennium of almost complete disuse) is clearly spelled out in the *General Instruction of the Roman Missal*:

> *In the general intercessions or prayer of the faithful, the people, exercising their priestly function, intercede for all humanity. It is appropriate that this prayer be included in all Masses celebrated with a congregation, so that prayers will be offered for the Church, for civil authorities, for those oppressed by various needs, for all people, and for the salvation of the world (GI #45).*

Implicit in the above is the sequence which should ordinarily be followed in formulating our intentions. Only after we have prayed for the needs of the Church as a whole and for the needs of the wider human community (especially the poor), do we place before God, from whom every good gift comes (Jas 1:17), our own needs as a parish. We can be quite specific, mentioning by name those who are ill and those who have died.

With a little creativity, it should not be difficult to relate the general intercessions to the readings of the day, the themes of the liturgical season, and the character of special occasions. Moreover, given their structure, they may sometimes (even for the sake of variety) be sung after the fashion of a litany.

Preparation of the Gifts

23 Liturgy of the Eucharist

On the eve of his passion, Jesus farewelled his disciples in the course of a Jewish ritual meal (probably the Passover). He invested the meal with new meaning and asked his followers to continue to do what he had done in memory of him (I Cor 11:24; Lk 22:19).

The shape of our liturgy of the Eucharist is basically that of the rite carried out by Jesus at the Last Supper. We take bread and wine; we give thanks; we break the bread; we consume the consecrated elements.

The terminology commonly used to describe this fourfold pattern is: the preparation of the gifts, the Eucharistic Prayer, the breaking of the bread, and the communion.

For some time the early Church continued the practice of celebrating the Eucharist in conjunction with an ordinary meal. This was no longer practical when the increasing size of congregations made it necessary to use public buildings rather than private homes for the service. Moreover, as Paul notes, certain abuses crept in which tended to obscure the true meaning of the assembly (I Cor 11:17-22). 'Your meetings for worship actually do more harm than good,' he wrote rather angrily to the Corinthian Church.

We come together not to offer another sacrifice which somehow parallels that of Jesus at the Last Supper and on Calvary. Our faith tells us that we unite ourselves with the very sacrifice Jesus, our high priest, offered 'once and for all' (Heb 7:27), perpetuating it 'throughout the ages until he [comes] again' (*SC* #47; cf. *GI* #48).

It is indeed a profound mystery that we enter into in our Sunday Mass.

24. Preparation of the altar

At the beginning of the liturgy of the Eucharist, our focus of attention shifts from the lectern and the ministers of the word to the altar and the presiding celebrant.

The altar, 'which is the centre of the whole eucharistic liturgy' (*GI* #49; cf. *GI* #262), is also referred to in official documents as 'the table of the Lord' (*GI #259*); for the Mass is both a sacrifice and a sacred meal. It is, as we noted earlier, deserving of our special respect.

The *General Instruction* requires that the altar be covered with at least one cloth (*GI #268*) and that there be a cross, 'clearly visible to the congregation, either on the altar or near it' (*GI #270*). The processional cross would satisfy this requirement well. Candlesticks are also to be placed on or around the altar (*GI #269*).

The more immediate preparation of the altar at this point in the Mass is entrusted to one of the ministers (usually an acolyte or an altar server) who, mindful of the sacred action which is about to be performed, places a corporal on it, together with the missal, the chalice(s) and the purificator(s). This activity, in itself, suggests that something new and important is about to happen.

Hopefully, all the above details are attended to with a minimum of fuss and with an eye to what Lucien Deiss calls 'festive tidiness'.

If we are distracted during these preparations, it is probably because at this time, in most parishes, the collection is taken up. This will be the subject of our next reflection.

25. The collection

The Law required each adult male Jew to pay a half-shekel annually towards the upkeep of the Temple (Ex 30:13-15) — an obligation which Jesus himself fulfilled (Mt 17:24-27). It was also customary for visitors to the Temple to contribute according to their means (Mk 12:41-44 — the widow's mite).

The early Christians, who had remained faithful to these practices of piety until their expulsion from the synagogues (c. 90 A.D.), were loath to come empty-handed to their celebration of the

Eucharist. They brought not only the bread and wine that were needed for worship but also food, clothing, money, and other necessities of life for distribution among the poor, the afflicted, and sojourners.

There were good precedents for this charitable concern. For example, Paul, writing ahead to the Christians in Corinth on behalf of the Church in Jerusalem, remarks: 'Every Sunday each of you must put aside some money, in proportion to what he has earned, and save it up, so that there will be no need to collect money when I come' (I Cor 16:2; cf. Rom 15:25-28; Acts 11:27-30)

Unfortunately, money is the only gift collected these days in most churches (cf. *GI* #49). We thereby miss a good opportunity to redistribute among our less fortunate sisters and brothers in Christ those superfluities which, according to the Fathers of the Church, rightfully belong to the poor.

Our giving in a context of worship will be more meaningful if it requires some sacrifice on our part and if it bespeaks an acknowledgement of the fact that all we have is gift from God. 'All we own we owe.' (Abraham Heschel).

26. Procession with the gifts

Though liturgical customs varied, we know that, in some places, Christians of the first centuries carried their gifts in procession to the altar, singing as they went.

This practice died out in the early Middle Ages with the general decline in congregational participation in the Mass (including the reception of the Eucharist) and the increasing use of unleavened bread. In our own day, however, as one of the minor fruits of the liturgical reform, the procession with the gifts has been restored.

We no longer bring the bread and wine for the liturgy from our own homes; but 'the rite of carrying up the gifts retains the same spiritual value and meaning' (*GI* #49). In this way we signify our intention to unite ourselves as a worshipping community with the sacred action which takes place at the altar. This procession will be balanced later by the communion procession when we receive these same gifts wondrously transformed.

Concerning the hymn, which has been restored along with the procession, the *General Instruction* has this to say: 'The procession bringing the gifts is accompanied by the presentation song, which continues at least until the gifts have been placed on the altar' (*GI* #50). Its function is 'to accompany and celebrate the communal aspects of the procession' (*MCW* #71).

The hymn need not speak of bread and wine or of offering in order to be considered appropriate. Indeed the hymn might be omitted altogether in favour of organ or instrumental music or, at times, a reverent silence.

27. Bread and wine

When we celebrate the Eucharist 'in memory of him', we use those elements which Jesus himself chose as symbols of his self-giving — bread and wine.

This symbolism is strikingly appropriate inasmuch as food surrenders, as it were, its own existence to promote life and growth in other creatures of God. Moreover, as the fruits of human labour, the bread and wine enable us to bring our daily lives into the mystery we celebrate.

Current legislation in the Latin Church requires us to use recently baked, unleavened wheaten bread (*GI* #282, 285). Ideally, it should be baked so that it looks like food and can be easily broken for distribution among the faithful (*GI* #283, 285). For practical reasons, we commonly use small individual wafers; but, in doing so, we tend to obscure the beautiful symbolism of sharing from the same loaf (see 1 Cor 10:16-17).

For the Jews, wine was a sign of festive joy and of stability in their own land. In Jesus' day, they followed the Greek custom of diluting their wine with water. Presumably, Jesus did so at the Last Supper.

Among Christians, this traditional practice has been variously interpreted. Whereas in the East it suggested the two natures in Jesus, it was seen in the West as symbolising the union of Christ and the baptised. For our part, we may also consider it as embodying our wish to unite ourselves with Christ's sacrifice in the Mass.

The wine that we use must be the fruit of the vine — natural, pure and unadulterated (*GI* #284-285).

28. Prayers at the preparation of the gifts

The prayers at what we used to call the offertory have been revised in such a way that we are left in no doubt that the offertory of the Mass takes place not here but during the Eucharistic Prayer (cf. *GI* #55f). This is why we have been speaking about the 'presentation' and 'preparation' of the gifts rather than about the 'offering' of them.

The two prayers of grateful praise, which the priest says either silently or audibly (depending on whether there is singing at this time and on local custom), are modelled on traditional Jewish table prayers (*berakoth*).

Raising the paten with the bread a little above the altar, the celebrant first praises the Creator God through whose providence we are able to offer the fruit of our toil which will become our bread of life (cf. *GI* #102).

Then having poured some wine and a little water into the chalice while saying an accompanying prayer softly, the priest holds the chalice above the altar and prays the second of the blessing prayers (cf. *GI* #103):

> *Blessed are you, Lord God of all creation. Through your goodness we have this wine to offer, fruit of the vine and work of human hands. It will become our spiritual drink.*

To these blessing prayers the congregation may respond (again according to local custom): 'Blessed be God forever.'

At this point, in solemn celebrations, the bread and wine and the priest and the assembled faith community may be incensed. The celebrant himself incenses the gifts (*GI* #105) and the deacon or other minister incenses the priest and the people (*GI* #133).

29. Washing the priest's hands

Having praised the Creator God for the gifts of bread and wine that will become our spiritual food and drink, the priest reflects briefly on the dispositions needed for one who would presume to celebrate the Lord's Supper. He prays:

Lord God, we ask you to receive us and be pleased with the sacrifice we offer you with humble and contrite hearts.

And, as his hands are washed, he adds a verse from the psalm we call the *Miserere:* 'Lord, wash

away my iniquity; cleanse me from my sin'
(Ps 51:2).

These prayers are said quietly by the priest because they form part of his own personal preparation for the sacred mysteries (*GI* #13, 106).

Centuries ago, when the faithful brought a variety
of gifts to the altar, the washing of the celebrant's
hands may have served a practical purpose. Today,
however, unless the priest has just incensed the
altar and the bread and wine, it is essentially a
symbolic gesture signifying one's need for inner
cleansing and purity of heart (*GI* #52).

The sprinkling of the people with holy water before the Mass in a rite known as the *Asperges*,
though its reference is more specifically baptis-
mal, may serve a similar purpose for the faithful
as a whole.

As any student of religion would know, ceremonial washings of one kind or another are
common in many religious traditions. They were
practised in the early Church and, as the scripture attests, in Jesus' own day. The reader may
recall the criticism that the scribes and Pharisees
levelled at Jesus for allowing his disciples to eat
with unwashed hands (Mk 7:1-5).

71

30. Invitation to prayer/ prayer over the gifts

With arms extended, the priest now invites us to pray that the sacrifice we are about to offer 'may be acceptable to God, the almighty Father' (cf. *GI* #53, 107). Our response (once entrusted to the altar servers) indicates our desire to participate in the sacred action, to praise and glorify God, and to enjoy the fruits of the Eucharist both as local faith community and as universal Church.

Originally, this invitation to prayer was addressed only to other members of the clergy present who responded in silence; but, in time, it was extended to the congregation as a whole.

The prayer over the gifts which follows this exchange is one of the presidential prayers we referred to earlier. It brings to a close the preparatory section of the liturgy of the Eucharist. We express our assent by acclaiming 'Amen' (cf. *GI* #107).

Prior to the post-conciliar liturgical reforms, it was customary for the celebrant to pray several prayers at this point in the Mass. He said them silently — hence the designation (which many readers will remember) 'secret prayers'.

In praying but one prayer over the gifts on the altar, and that audibly, we have reverted to the ancient Roman liturgical practice.

The structure of the prayer is simple: (i) we invoke God; (ii) we make an appropriate petition; and (iii) we conclude our prayer using one of the shorter formulas (cf. *GI* #32).

If the structure is predictable, so also is the content of the prayer which leads us very smoothly into the Eucharistic Prayer to which we now direct our attention.

Eucharistic Prayer

31. Eucharistic Prayer: background and origins

Traditional Jewish piety sought to sanctify the entire day with blessings to suit various activities. Especially relevant to our present topic are the blessings which accompanied the family meal.

At the beginning of the meal, the head of the household prayed a blessing over the bread which was then broken and shared among those at table. A similar blessing was prayed over the cup of wine at the conclusion of the meal.

It was not the food that was blessed but God, the giver of all good gifts. 'Blessed are you,' the father prayed, 'Lord, our God, king of the world, who has brought bread from heaven.'

The recurrent pattern of these Jewish blessings (*berakoth*), at least in their more developed form, is as follows: (a) an expression of grateful praise to God the Creator of all things; (b) a remembrance of God's saving interventions in the history of the people; (c) a plea that the beneficent God will continue to deal favourably with them; and (d) a concluding doxology (prayer of praise).

At the Last Supper, Jesus prayed the customary blessings, investing them with new meaning. Not only did he acknowledge the bread and wine as gifts of God, he also made them his own gifts to those present — sacramental signs of his saving presence to them until he should come again.

Mindful of Jesus' command that we should 'do this in memory of [him]' (Lk 22:19), we assemble to offer his sacrifice and to partake of his sacred body and blood. The 'centre and summit' of our celebration is the 'prayer of thanksgiving and sanctification' we call the Eucharistic Prayer (*GI* #54).

77

32. Eucharistic Prayer: structure and unity

It will become clearer that the Eucharistic Prayer is structured after the fashion of the Jewish prayer of blessing (*berakah*) if we identify the elements of which it is composed. These are listed in the *General Instruction of the Roman Missal* as follows: **thanksgiving** (especially, but not exclusively, in the preface); **acclamation** (in the *Sanctus*); **epiclesis** (an invocation that God the Father will send the Holy Spirit to sanctify our offerings); **narrative of institution**; **anamnesis** (a remembrance of the paschal mystery of

Jesus' passion, death, resurrection and ascension); **offering** (the offertory properly so called of the Mass); **intercessions** (prayers of supplication for the living and the dead); **final doxology** (a concluding prayer of praise to which the people respond 'Amen!'). (cf. *GI #55*).

In noting these elements, we must not overlook the ongoing rhythm of the Eucharistic Prayer and its internal unity as a prayer of praise and thanksgiving. It is within the Eucharistic Prayer that the specifically sacramental mode of the risen Lord's presence is effected.

The Eucharistic Prayer is known by several names, each of which highlights one of the elements listed above. We used to speak of it as the 'Canon of the Mass', from a Greek word suggesting something fixed or a standard to be followed. Occasionally the term 'anaphora' (from the Greek for offering or lifting up) is used, especially in the Eastern Church. In the Roman rite, however, we prefer the title 'Eucharistic Prayer' (Gk. *eucharistia* = thanksgiving).

In what follows we will look at some of these elements in more detail.

33. Preface/Sanctus

The Eucharistic Prayer begins appropriately with the preface — a joyful hymn of praise and thanksgiving in which (according to the feast, special occasion, or liturgical season) we recall different aspects of the mystery of salvation (*GI* #55a).

It is introduced by a dialogue between the people and the priest who invites us, with uplifted hearts, to unite with him as he prays in the name of the entire faith community (*GI* #108).

Today, thanks to the liturgical revisions following Vatican II, we have upwards of eighty prefaces. These are often linked thematically with the Gospel of the day, as a study of the Lenten prefaces, for example, would reveal. Like the readings and the homily, therefore, they also serve to proclaim the good news.

The preface leads smoothly into the *Sanctus* — an acclamation which recalls the vision of the prophet Isaiah in the Temple (Is 6:2-3; cf. Rev 4:8). This is one of the three acclamations which the people make during the Eucharistic Prayer (the others are the memorial acclamation and the Great Amen). In this way we identify with and, as it were, ratify what the celebrant does on our behalf in the name and power of Christ the Priest.

When we sing the *Sanctus* together (and surely it calls out to be sung), 'we join the whole communion of saints in acclaiming the Lord' (*MCW* #56).

The passage beginning 'Blessed be he . . .' calls to mind the people's greeting on the occasion of Jesus' triumphal entry into Jerusalem (Mt 21:9; cf. Ps 118:26).

34. Invocation of the Holy Spirit

Our observations in this essay relate most directly to the new Eucharistic Prayers (II, III, and IV) wherein the invocation of the Holy Spirit before the institution narrative is more explicit than it is in Eucharistic Prayer I (the 'Roman canon').

A study of the text of the Mass (which the reader is encouraged to make) will reveal that a prayer praising the Father serves as a link between the *Sanctus* and what liturgists call the **epiclesis** or, more simply, the invocation of the Spirit. In Eucharistic Prayer IV this prayer of praise is elaborated into a history of salvation.

The celebrant makes use of a very ancient gesture which we may recall from the day of our confirmation. He extends his hands over the bread and wine and prays that God the Father will send the Holy Spirit to sanctify our offerings so that 'they may become for us the body and blood of our Lord, Jesus Christ'.

In the first of the three Eucharistic Prayers for Masses with Children, we have a beautifully direct and expressive example of an epiclesis:

> *God, our Father, you are most holy and we want to show you that we are grateful. We bring you bread and wine and ask you to send your Holy Spirit to make these gifts the body and blood of Jesus Christ your Son. Then we can offer to you what you have given to us.*

Later (in Eucharistic Prayers II, III, and IV), after the memorial acclamation, we will again recall the sanctifying role of the Spirit by whose working 'all life, all holiness' come to us (cf. *EP* III).

35. Narrative of institution/ memorial acclamation

Even before the New Testament accounts were written down, the early Christians told the story of the institution of the Blessed Eucharist when they assembled for worship.

Following their example, we continue to tell the story today as an integral part of all our Eucharistic Prayers (cf. *GI* #55d), using the same words of institution in each case in slightly different narrative settings.

The celebrant performs some of the actions referred to in the text; others (for example, the breaking of the bread) are reserved for later. He also shows the eucharistic bread and the cup to the faithful and genuflects before the consecrated elements (*GI* #233). These gestures and the ringing of a bell at this time (*GI* #109) derive from an era when the Eucharistic Prayer was prayed silently and the people seldom received communion.

As we listen to the narrative, we should be aware that it is not just a recounting of ancient events; it is a solemn proclamation of the saving mystery which is here and now being accomplished in our midst (*SC* #47).

This is the 'mystery of faith' which we acclaim in response to the invitation of the priest or deacon, 'Let us proclaim the mystery of faith.' We are affirming much more than our belief in the real presence of Jesus Christ in what appears to be but bread and wine. In the words of the U.S. bishops: 'We support one another's faith in the paschal mystery, the central mystery of our belief. The acclamation is properly a memorial of the Lord's suffering and glorification, with an expression of faith in his coming' (*MCW* #57).

This memorial acclamation should also serve to refocus our attention, should that be necessary.

36. Anamnesis
(memorial prayer)

'Much of what the Bible commands,' wrote Rabbi Abraham Heschel, 'can be comprised in one word, "Remember".' This insight colours the entire prayer life of the Jewish people.

Especially at Passover time, they recall with praise and thanksgiving the wonderful interventions of God in their history (see Deut 8; Ex 12: 1-28). They are deeply aware that the ceremonial remembrance of these saving events makes them present in a mysterious way, enabling the people to enjoy the continuing fruitfulness of God's saving action.

A like awareness should inform our celebration of the Eucharist in response to Jesus' command, 'Do this in memory of me' (Lk 22:19; cf. 1 Cor 11:25).The Mass does not just recall the sacrifice of Jesus; it is itself a sacrifice — the same sacrifice as that of Jesus, sacramentally actualised for us people and for our salvation (cf. *SC* #47; 102).

As the whole Mass is the memorial of the passion, resurrection and ascension of Jesus Christ, it might seem almost superfluous to include this explicit remembrance in the Eucharistic Prayer, the more so as it follows the narrative of institution and memorial acclamation. However, there are good historical grounds for doing so; and it leads very naturally into the offering of 'the spotless victim to the Father in the Holy Spirit' (*GI* #55f).

The anamnesis, or memorial prayer, varies from one Eucharistic Prayer to another. A little more extensive than the others is the one in Eucharistic Prayer IV which not only recalls past aspects of the paschal mystery but also looks forward to our Lord's second coming.

37. Offering

In all the Eucharistic Prayers there is a prayer of offering. Linked to the anamnesis (the memorial prayer), it is, as we noted earlier, the offertory properly so-called of the Mass.

In this connection we need to ask ourselves the following questions: To whom is the offering made? What/who is offered? Who makes the offering? To what ends is the offering made? The answers are clearly given in the various Eucharistic Prayers.

In every case the prayer of offering is addressed to the Father. We offer 'this holy and perfect sacrifice: the bread of life and the cup of eternal salvation' (*EP* I); the 'body and blood [of Jesus], the acceptable sacrifice which brings salvation to the whole world' (*EP* IV).

Moreover, as the *General Instruction* states, 'The Church's intention is that the faithful not only offer this victim but also learn to offer themselves ...' (*GI* #55f; cf, *SC* #48). This offering of ourselves 'as a living sacrifice to God, dedicated to his service and pleasing to him' is, according to St Paul, 'the true worship that [we] should offer' (Rom 12:1).

It is the whole Church which makes the offering of 'the spotless victim'. In a given time and place the universal Church is represented by the community which assembles to celebrate the Eucharist (*GI* #55f; 74-75).

We make our offering to give praise and thanksgiving to God and so that we may be 'filled with every grace and blessing' (*EP* I). We wish to be 'brought together in unity by the Holy Spirit' (*EP* II) as 'the one body of Christ' (*EP* IV).

38. Intercessions

The Hebrew Scriptures provide many examples of great leaders who interceded with God on behalf of their sinful people (see Gen 18:16-33; 20:14-17; Deut 9:18-29).

This tradition of intercessory prayer, which finds expression in the Jewish prayer of blessing over the cup, may have influenced the liturgical formulas of the early Christian Church.

Christians came to believe that there is one intercessor who brings the merciful God and needy humankind together in a unique and enduringly efficacious way — 'the man Christ Jesus, who gave himself to redeem all humanity' (1 Tim 2: 5-6). He is the supreme High Priest (Heb 8:1-6).

In the Eucharistic Prayer, not surprisingly, after we have united ourselves with Jesus in offering his perfect sacrifice to the Father, we pray 'for the Church and all its members, living and dead, who are called to share in the salvation and redemption purchased by Christ's body and blood' (*GI* #55g).

The arrangement of these intercessory prayers varies in the different Eucharistic Prayers. In the first of these (the 'Roman canon') there are two groups of intercessions — one before the institution narrative and one after it. This Eucharistic Prayer also includes two lists of apostles and martyrs specially venerated in Rome — a reminder to us that we celebrate 'in union with the whole Church', including those who 'have gone before us marked with the sign of faith' (*EP* I) and 'on whose constant intercession we rely for help' (*EP* III).

We pray especially that, like them, we will some day enjoy the fruits of Christ's sacrifice at the heavenly banquet.

39. Final doxology/great Amen

In the spirit of the Jewish *berakah* tradition, the Eucharistic Prayer is always brought to a fittingly climactic conclusion with a doxology. Thus it ends as it began — on a note of jubilant praise of the Father.

As the priest (not the people — *GI #*55h) recites or sings the Trinitarian doxology, 'Through him, with him, in him . . .', he elevates the consecrated bread and wine in a gesture of offering.

We, who have listened to the Eucharistic Prayer 'in silent reverence' (*GI* #55), respond with a resounding 'Amen' (cf. Rev 1:6-7; 5:14; 19:4; 2 Cor 1:20). Describing the Christian Eucharist in the middle of the second century, the martyr Justin noted: 'When the prayer of thanksgiving is ended, all the people present give their assent with an 'Amen' ('Amen' in Hebrew means 'So be it')' (*First Apology* 65, 3-4).

This is the third acclamation that we make during the Eucharistic Prayer (the others are the *Sanctus* and the memorial acclamation after the institution narrative). It is our way of affirming (perhaps even ratifying) all that has been prayed in our name by the priest in the Eucharistic Prayer.

Like all acclamations, it should be shouted or, better still, sung with enthusiasm. However, as it is not easy to sing a word of two syllables effectively, 'the Amen may be repeated or augmented. Choirs may harmonize and expand upon the people's acclamation' (*MCW* #58). We need not aim at the heights that Handel scaled in the finale to his *Messiah*.

In the essays which follow, we will turn our attention to the Communion Rite.

Communion Rite

40. Communion rite

Since the eucharistic celebration is the paschal meal, it is right that the faithful who are properly disposed receive the Lord's body and blood as spiritual food as he commanded. This is the purpose of the breaking of the bread and the other preparatory rites that lead directly to the communion of the people (GI #56).

The practice of the early Christians was to proceed directly from the Eucharistic Prayer to the breaking of the bread and communion under both kinds. As time went by, a more elaborate communion rite developed which was designed to assist the participants in their immediate preparation for the reception of the Sacrament.

Today, after some necessary liturgical reforms, this rite consists of: the Lord's Prayer, the rite of peace, the breaking of the bread, and the holy communion.

A study of these four elements will reveal our concern that we approach the Lord's table with the best possible dispositions.

Understandably, there is emphasis on the need for reconciliation, forgiveness, and the unity in love that should characterise Jesus' disciples (cf. Jn 13:35). 'The first fruit of the Eucharist is the unity of the Body of Christ, Christians being loved by Christ and loving him through their love of one another' (*MCW* #48; cf. 1 Cor 10:16-17).

We acknowledge once again our sinfulness, our need for forgiveness, and our unworthiness to participate in so great a mystery in which we 'proclaim the Lord's death until he comes' (1 Cor 11:26).

As distractions come easily to most of us, we need to pause and remind ourselves occasionally of the purpose of this rite and enter into it as fully as possible.

41. Lord's Prayer/doxology

The Lord's Prayer was introduced into the Mass after the breaking of the bread (as in the Eastern Church today) towards the end of the fourth century. Its present position in the Roman liturgy dates from the liturgical reform of Pope St Gregory the Great two centuries later.

Originally in Rome, it was said or sung only by the priest. Today, however, as a result of continuing liturgical reform, it is quite rightly a part of the Mass that is 'assigned to the whole congregation' (*GI* #16). 'The priest offers the invitation to pray, but the faithful say [or sing] the prayer with him' (*GI* #56a).

The *Our Father* (cf. Mt 6:9-13) begins our immediate preparation for the holy communion. It is an appropriate prayer for this purpose as it combines praise of our heavenly Father with pertinent intercessions. We wish to approach the table of our Lord with hearts free from sin and in a spirit of love and mutual harmony.

In what is called the *embolism*, the priest expands upon our plea to be delivered from evil by praying that we might enjoy 'peace in our day'. The peace in question is the wholeness/holiness of the person who seeks to do God's will. As Dante wisely observed, 'In his will is our peace.'

We who 'wait in joyful hope' will know complete peace only with 'the coming of our Saviour, Jesus Christ' (cf. Tit 2:13).

The acclamation, 'For the kingdom ...' (cf. I Chron 29:11), is a doxology which has been associated with the recitation of the Lord's Prayer from the earliest times (cf. Didache 8:2). It may be 'fittingly sung by all' (*MCW* #59).

42. Sign of peace

The sign of peace, the second element in our communion rite, derives from the 'holy kiss' (Rom 16:16; 1 Cor 16:20; 2 Cor 13:12; 1 Thess 5:26) or the 'kiss of Christian love' (1 Pet 5:14) which the early Christians were encouraged to exchange among themselves.

In many liturgies it is to be found immediately before the presentation of the gifts, in keeping with our Lord's injunction that we should be reconciled with one another before bringing our gifts to the altar (Mt 5:23-24; Mk 11:25; *Didache* 14:1-2).

The Roman practice, at least from the time of Pope Innocent I (401-417), has been to exchange the sign of peace before receiving Christ's body and blood in holy communion.

Across the centuries the ceremonial expression of this sign of reconciliation has varied from place to place. Eventually it was restricted to those who were to receive communion, which in practice meant the clergy; but, since 1969, this beautiful 'sign of [our] love for one another' (*GI* #56b) has been reintroduced for all the faithful.

Addressing our Lord Jesus Christ (prayers in the Mass are usually directed to the Father), the priest prays with hands extended for 'the peace and unity of [his] kingdom'. Then, having exchanged a greeting with us, the priest (or the deacon — *GI* #136, 194) invites us to 'offer each other the sign of peace'.

To offer peace to others (in the sense of the Hebrew word *shalom*) is to pray that they will enjoy harmony in their relationships; it is the peace that was Jesus' special gift to his own at the Last Supper (Jn 14:27).

43. Breaking of the bread

All four accounts of the institution of the Blessed Eucharist record that Jesus, in accordance with Jewish custom, broke bread at the Last Supper. This traditional practice acquired special meaning for the early Christian Church which designated its eucharistic celebration as 'the breaking of bread' (Acts 2:42, 46; 20:7, 11 JB; *GI* #56c; 283). It was the sign in which the disciples at Emmaus knew their risen Lord (Lk 24:30-31,35).

The breaking of the single consecrated loaf was more than just a practical necessity; it was pregnant with symbolism. In Paul's words: 'Because there is the one loaf of bread, all of us, though many, are one body, for we all share the same loaf' (1 Cor 10:17)

A like understanding is expressed in the much quoted passage from the *Didache*, a mid-second century document: 'As this broken bread was scattered over the mountain and when brought together became one, so let your Church be brought together from the ends of the earth into your kingdom' (*Didache* 9:3)

With the mandatory use of unleavened bread and the introduction of small wafers for the people, this symbolism was lost for a millennium. Fortunately, it is being reclaimed in many places today.

The *General Instruction* reminds us 'that the nature of the sign demands that the material for the eucharistic celebration truly have the appearance of food' (*GI* #283). At the same time, however, care must be taken in preparing the ingredients (wheaten flour and water) 'to ensure that the product does not detract from the dignity due to the Eucharistic bread' (*ID* #8).

44. Commingling/Agnus Dei

Having broken the host over the paten, the celebrant places a small portion of it in the chalice, saying quietly: 'May this mingling of the body and blood of our Lord Jesus Christ bring eternal life to us who receive it' (cf. *GI* #56d and #113).

There is a long and rather complicated history behind this gesture, the significance of which has been variously understood. It was introduced into the Roman liturgy by a pope of Syrian origin during the eighth century.

The bringing together of the consecrated elements was seen by some Christians as signifying the resurrection of Christ, just as the separate consecration of the bread and wine symbolised his sacrificial death.

During the breaking of the bread, we recite, or preferably sing, the *Agnus Dei* (*GI* #56e and #113; *MCW* #68). The invocation and its accompanying response are commonly said three times; but the *Agnus Dei* may be repeated until the breaking of the bread is complete. As it is a litany-song, it can be sung to good effect by a choir with the congregation singing the response.

The *Agnus Dei*, which is also derived from Syrian sources, recalls the words of John the Baptist to his followers. Having denied that he was the long-awaited Messiah or Elijah or the Prophet, John pointed to Jesus and said: 'There is the Lamb of God, who takes away the sin of the world!' (Jn 1:29; cf. 1:36).

We may take it as referring to Christ, the true Passover Lamb (1 Cor 5:7; Jn 19:36), who conquered death (Rev 5:6-14; 13:8) in the sacrificial offering of his own life (Is 53:6-7).

45. Communion preparation/ invitation

As his own personal and immediate preparation for holy communion, the celebrant prays (in a low voice and with his hands joined) one of two prayers so that 'he may receive Christ's body and blood to good effect' (*GI* #56f; cf. #13). If we wish, we can make these prayers our own; or we can pray in the quiet of our hearts as the Spirit moves.

The priest then genuflects and, holding the broken eucharistic bread slightly above the paten, shows it to the people (*GI* #56g; #115). By way of inviting us to share in the holy communion, he prays aloud: 'This is the Lamb of God who takes away the sins of the world. Happy are those who are called to his supper' (cf. Jn 1:29, 36; Rev 19:9).

This is in fact a double invitation; for it refers not only to the eucharistic banquet but also to 'the wedding feast of the Lamb'. The nourishment we take at the table of the Lord is our 'pledge of future glory' (*SC* #47).

Again drawing on the words of sacred scripture, the priest and people say together, with a small variation, the words of the humble Roman centurion: 'Lord, I am not worthy . . .' (Mt 8:8; cf. Lk 5:8).

In passing, we may note that a formal invitation to communion is part of most Christian eucharistic liturgies.

Our present rite is, as older members of the congregation will know, much simpler than the one which obtained in the days before the Council when the priest and people separately prayed the 'Lord, I am not worthy . . .' (three times each) and recited in addition the *Confiteor*. How times have changed!

46. Communion procession/ song

We need to remind ourselves from time to time that we do not simply join a queue to receive communion. We take part, with other members of the faith community, in a procession to the Lord's table. This is one of four processions in the Mass; and, like the others, it is usually accompanied by a song (*GI* #22; *EAW* #59).

Even as far back as the time of St Augustine (354-430) it was customary for the people to process to the altar while singing a suitable psalm (for example, Psalm 34). However, when frequent communion became the exception rather than the rule, only the antiphon was sung.

Today, happily, the practice of singing the communion song has been restored. It is begun while the priest is receiving the sacrament (*GI #56i; #119*). If it is not sung, the communion antiphon in the missal may be recited.

Appropriate psalms may be chosen or hymns (perhaps seasonal in character) which point to our joy in receiving the Blessed Eucharist and our unity in faith and love with one another.

The function of this song, which should ordinarily be simple enough for all to join in, is clearly spelled out in the *General Instruction:* '[It] expresses the spiritual union of the communicants who join their voices in a single song, shows the joy of all, and makes the communion procession an act of brotherhood [and sisterhood]' (*GI #56i; cf. MCW #62*).

It is well not to extend this song for too long, especially if there is to be more singing after the communion. An instrumental interlude could sometimes be considered by way of variation (*MCW #37*).

47. Reception of communion

The first to receive communion is the priest, who having prayed quietly to be brought to everlasting life, reverently consumes the body and blood of Christ (*GI #116*).

When we receive communion, the eucharistic minister holds the consecrated host before us and says, 'The body of Christ' — to which we reply 'Amen' (*GI #117*). A similar procedure is followed with the chalice if communion is to be received under both kinds.

Our 'Amen' is an act of faith in the Real Presence; it is also an acknowledgement that we are the Mystical Body of Christ (cf. 1 Cor 12:27). As St Augustine says, 'It is your very own mystery which is laid upon the Lord's table.'

In the early Church, communion was received standing. This has become once again the more general practice today. If we do not communicate kneeling, 'it is strongly recommended that ... [we] should make a sign of reverence [e.g. a genuflection] before receiving the sacrament' (*ID* #11).

The practice of receiving communion in the hand has also been reintroduced; but it is not of obligation. This was customary until the ninth or tenth century. In a well-known quotation St Cyril of Jerusalem says: 'When you approach, do not go stretching out your hands or having your fingers spread out, but make the left hand into a throne for the right which shall receive the King.'

Yet another reform has seen the reintroduction of communion under both kinds for the faithful (*SC* #55; *GI* #56; #240-242) — an initiative that has ecumenical significance. 'Holy communion has a more complete form as a sign when it is received under both kinds' (*GI* #240).

111

48. Prayer after communion

Provision has been made in the Mass for brief periods of silent, prayerful reflection (*SC* #30; *GI* #23). One of the most important of these is the very intimate time after the reception of communion when we are especially aware of the presence of the Lord in ourselves personally and in the community. 'Whoever eats my flesh,' said

Jesus, 'and drinks my blood lives in me, and I live in him' (Jn 6:56).

If it thought desirable, the congregation may sing a 'hymn, psalm, or other song of praise' at this time (*GI* #56j; *MCW* #72). It is not intended that this replace the time of silence.

The communion rite comes to a close with the recitation by the priest of what is now called the prayer after communion. Standing with arms outstretched either at the altar or the chair (*GI* #122; #56k), he prays this presidential prayer on our behalf; and we make it our own by responding, 'Amen'.

Note that this is not a prayer of thanksgiving (the Eucharistic Prayer adequately serves that purpose) but a plea that the sacrament we have received will be fruitful in our lives (*GI* #56k). The prayer after communion for the Solemnity of Corpus Christi beautifully illustrates this: 'Lord Jesus Christ, you give us your body and blood in the eucharist as a sign that even now we share your life. May we come to possess it completely in the kingdom where you live for ever and ever.'

All that now remains is the concluding rite to which we will next turn our attention.

sus, and drinks my blood lives in me, and I live in him." (Jn 6:56).

If it thought desirable, the congregation may sing a hymn, psalm, or other song of praise, at this time (GI #56; MCW #72). It is not intended that this replace the time of silence.

The communion rite comes to a close with the recitation by the priest of what is now called the prayer after communion. Standing, with arms outstretched either at the altar or the chair (GI #122; #56f), he prays this (presidential) prayer on our behalf; and we make it our own by responding, Amen.

Note that this is not a prayer of thanksgiving (the Eucharistic Prayer adequately serves that purpose) but a plea that the sacrament we have received will be fruitful in our lives (GI #56f). The prayer after communion for the Solemnity of Corpus Christi beautifully illustrates this: Lord Jesus Christ, you give us your body and blood in the eucharist as a sign that even now we share your life. May we come to possess it completely in the kingdom where you live for ever and ever.

All that now remains is the concluding rite to which we will now turn our attention.

Concluding Rite

49. Concluding rite

The early Church's practice of ending the Mass with the distribution of communion gave way in time to an increasingly elaborate concluding rite which, as older Catholics would remember, included a reading of the prologue of St John's Gospel.

At the Second Vatican Council, the bishops called for a revision of the Mass. Those parts 'which with the passage of time came to be duplicated, or were added with little advantage' (*SC* #50) were to be omitted.

As a result, the concluding rite has been simplified and improved so that it now appears more clearly as 'one continuous action' (*MCW* #49) comprising the priest's greeting and blessing and the formal dismissal of the assembly (cf. *GI* #57).

When another liturgical service follows the Mass, the concluding rite is omitted (*GI* #126). This most commonly happens when a funeral Mass is directly joined to the burial (*GI* #340). It is also the case on Holy Thursday when, following the prayer after communion, there is a eucharistic procession.

If there are parish notices to be made, they should be given at the beginning of the concluding rite (*GI* #123). This is preferable to inserting them after the homily when they would be rather distracting to people's reflection on the readings of the day.

Announcements of this kind should be brief and of general interest. To preserve its special character, the ambo should not be used for this purpose (*GI* #272; *EAW* 74-75).

50. Final blessing

At the end of his Gospel, St Luke records that Jesus raised his hands and blessed his disciples; and 'as he was blessing them, he departed from them and was taken up into heaven' (Lk 24:51).

The Church, which continues to bless in Jesus' name and in the power of his Spirit, concludes its memorial celebration of his paschal mystery with a blessing.

With outstretched hands, the priest first greets the people as he did at the beginning of the Mass. After our response, he blesses all present with the sign of the cross (*GI #57; #124*). We answer, 'Amen.'

The simplest form of the blessing is: 'May almighty God bless you, the Father, and the Son, and the Holy Spirit.' However, 'on certain days and occasions', a more solemn form may be used. In this case, the celebrant (or the deacon) invites us to bow our heads and reads a blessing which may reflect the character of a particular feast or of the liturgical season. To each of its invocations we respond, 'Amen'; and the priest concludes with the words given above.

The sacramentary also provides for the inclusion in the final blessing of a 'prayer over the people'. Examples of these may be found by turning to the Sundays of Lent in your missal.

The blessing is a prayer that God, from whom we have just received the greatest of all gifts, will continue to grace us with his abiding presence in our daily lives (cf. Mt 28:20).

51. Dismissal

A formal dismissal at the end of Mass is to be found in almost all traditional eucharistic liturgies. It is said or sung by a deacon if one is present (*GI #140*).

The sacramentary gives three dismissal formulas, all of which direct the faithful to 'go in peace' (cf. Mk 5:34; Lk 7:50). Our response in each case is, 'Thanks be to God.'

The dismissal is not just a sending away but a sending forth. Just as the entrance rite highlights the fact that we come together in holy fellowship, so also the concluding rite commissions the assembly to extend that fellowship by lives of love and service which witness to the good news of Jesus Risen (cf. Mt 28:19-20).

After the dismissal, the priest kisses the altar (as he did in the introductory rite) and, having made the proper reverence with the other ministers, leaves the sanctuary (*GI* #125; #141; 233-234).

A recessional hymn may be sung by the congregation. 'However, if the people have sung a song after communion, it may be advisable to use only an instrumental or choir recessional' (*MCW* #73). If there is a hymn at the end of the Mass, it should be not only 'eucharistic' but also 'in keeping ... with the feast, or with the liturgical season' (*MS* #36).

The Mass is ended; but, as Fr Pedro Arrupe reminds us, our celebration of the Christian Eucharist will always remain incomplete while Christ continues to suffer in the poor of this world who lack the daily bread which so many of us just take for granted.

Appendix:

Arrangement of readings for Sunday Masses

Each Sunday Mass has three scripture readings: the first from the Old Testament (or the Acts of the Apostles during the Easter season); the second from an apostle (or the Book of Revelation); and the third from the Gospels.

A three year cycle of readings is followed for Sundays. In Year A the Gospel of Matthew is read; in Year B the Gospel of Mark, and John chapter 6 (the sermon on 'the Bread of Life'). Year C is the year of Luke.

The Old Testament readings follow no pattern but are selected to reveal the harmony between the Old and New Testaments. The readings chosen address similar themes to the New Testament texts read in the same Mass, particularly the Gospel text.

There is a systematic reading of the New Testament letters, as set out on the next page.

Arrangement of the second reading for the Sundays in Ordinary Time

Sunday	Year A	Year B	Year C
2	1 Corinthians 1-4	1 Corinthians 6-11	1 Corinthians 12-15
3	,,	,,	,,
4	,,	,,	,,
5	,,	,,	,,
6	,,	,,	,,
7	,,	2 Corinthians	,,
8	,,	,,	,,
9	Romans	,,	Galatians
10	,,	,,	,,
11	,,	,,	,,
12	,,	,,	,,
13	,,	,,	,,
14	,,	,,	,,
15	,,	Ephesians	Colossians
16	,,	,,	,,
17	,,	,,	,,
18	,,	,,	,,
19	,,	,,	Hebrews 11-12
20	,,	,,	,,
21	,,	,,	,,
22	,,	James	,,
23	,,	,,	Philemon
24	,,	,,	1 Timothy
25	Philippians	,,	,,
26	,,	,,	,,
27	,,	Hebrews 2-10	2 Timothy
28	,,	,,	,,
29	1 Thessalonians	,,	,,
30	,,	,,	,,
31	,,	,,	2 Thessalonians
32	,,	,,	,,
33	,,	,,	,,

123

Abbreviations

DMC   Congregation for Divine Worship, *Directory for Masses with Children (Pueros baptizatos)*, 1973.

DV   Vatican Council II, *Dogmatic Constitution on Divine Revelation (Dei verbum)*, 1965.

EAW   Bishops' Committee on the Liturgy (U.S.) *Environment and Art in Catholic Worship*, 1978.

GI   Congregation for Divine Worship, *General Instruction of the Roman Missal*, fourth edition 1975.

GS   Vatican Council II, *Pastoral Constitution on the Church in the Modern World (Gaudium et spes)*, 1965.

ID   Congregation for the Sacraments and Divine Worship, instruction *Inaestimabile Donum*, 1980.

LMI   Congregation for the Sacraments and Divine Worship, *Lectionary for Mass: Introduction*, second *editio typica* 1981.

MCW   Bishops' Committee on the Liturgy (U.S.), *Music in Catholic Worship*, revised edition 1983.

MF   Pope Paul VI, encyclical letter *Mysterium Fidei,* 1965.

MS   Congregation of Rites, *Instruction on Music in the Liturgy (Musicam sacram),* 1967.

SC   Vatican Council II, *Constitution on the Sacred Liturgy (Sacrosanctum Concilium),* 1963.

Faith and Prayer Education Series

A collection of popular titles intended to help adults and secondary school students to better understand their faith, and grow in their life of prayer. Titles in the series so far: